RED EPIC

∞

COMMUNE EDITIONS

Red Epic, Joshua Clover
We Are Nothing and So Can You, Jasper Bernes
That Winter the Wolf Came, Juliana Spahr

Red Epic

JOSHUA CLOVER

∞

Commune Editions
Oakland, California (communeeditions@gmail.com)

An imprint of AK Press / AK Press UK
Oakland, California (akpress@akpress.org)
Edinburgh, Scotland (ak@akedin.demon.co.uk)

Cover illustration and Commune Editions design by Front Group Design
  (frontgroupdesign.com)

Library of Congress Cataloging-in-Publication Data

Clover, Joshua
  Red epic / Joshua Clover

  ISBN 978-1-934639-16-0 (pbk.: alk. paper)
  Library of Congress Control Number: 2014958775

Printed on acid-free paper by McNaughton & Gunn, Michigan, U.S.A. The paper
  used in this publication meets the minimum requirements of ANSI/NISO Z39.48-
  1992 (R2009) (*Permanence of Paper*).

FOR COMRADES

TABLE OF CONTENTS

My Life in the New Millennium   3
Years of Analysis for a Day of Synthesis   5
The Fire Sermon   10
Tranche I   16
Tranche II   17
Haecceity   18
Spring Georgic   19
The Transformation Problem   23
Little Object Andy   28
Poem (Polis is metro polis is akros)   29
Gilded Age   30
Poem (It was raining in das Kapital)   33
Poem (We lived in a cloud of recklessness)   35
The Event   36
Fab, Beta, Equity Vol   38
Galactic   43
Poem (In the city it was warmer)   45
Poem (This town is going out of business)   47
Apology   48
Omnibus Omnia   50

The Red Posters   52

Memories of Bergen op Zoom   53

Poem (Stop it with your strategies)   55

Le Mépris   56

Contempt   57

LTCM   58

Metalipsis for Uyen Hua   68

Questions of the Contemporary   69

Acknowledgments   75

...remember
you can have what you ask for, ask for
everything

My Life in the New Millennium

It was true that the more I hated people the more I loved cats.
Then people started to surprise me.
Often this involved fire or Coca-Cola
bottles with petrol which amounts to the same thing.
Once fire is the form of the spectacle the problem
becomes how to set fire to fire.
Some friends were prepared to help with this which
Michael Jackson having died and then Whitney Houston
was the new pop music. Without an understanding
of the world system and the underlying truth of land
as the place of politics and the sea as the space of commerce
it is hard to integrate that other
most important fact of our era. Pirates. My friends
and pirates and cats—it comes down
to comrades known and elsewhere.

Years of Analysis for a Day of Synthesis

Real city! I am always arriving
                 elsewhere having traversed
                             the threshold of the century
and still trapped
              in the approximations
                      of the lyric or the post-lyric or the lyric
with Chinese characteristics
                  super-guanxi post '78
                        period style for the vita nuova-
esque situation that devised
                the rhizome and the chaebol
                          and Paper Planes
and Paper Planes Diplo Remix
                  featuring Bun B and Rich Boy
                        and O…Saya
and Paper Planes DFA Remix
                  and the century was shit
                       but the acoustics were awesome
and you could hear the human
                  poets sing economy
                      of language while paring
the poem down to an object
                  oriented ontology subhed Parmenides
                       among the Moderns

but surely we are forgiven

        for hardening our strophes

                against the marketplace

in an epoch whose novelty lies

        in the precise arrangement of its word

                cloud titrated forth

from other epochs and after all

        one traverses an era

                as one passes the Dogana point

that is to say rather quickly

        and heads out to open water

                swiftly losing sight

of the Customs House steps

        with fareless bearded loiterer

                but still unable to arrive

at the end of the sentence

        where words realize their meaning

                except to hurry on

and this restless motion marks

        the adventure of value

                set loose in the circuits

and unable to know itself

        without arriving headlong

                at the price briefly valorized

a pause eros a sum on paper

        then crashing onward

                into the orbits sweet

with longing like Francesca

        circling immaterial

                through the fifth Canto

able to fling a phrase

        or two at most before hurrying on

                and the truth of this rests

not in her words

        but the peregrination of Francesca

                the Comedian as the letter C

in the general formula MCM′

        that crawled ashore on the sea

                flecked lip

of the world
        system not far from Rimini
                where Francesca died and Sigismondo
lived and died
        but across the peninsula
                at the Casa San Giorgio with its rule
so discreet and sophisticated
             that historians for a long time
                    failed to notice it
but it was here the young formula
             for does not every formula
                    deserve a childhood
here it came of age
        and then went down to the ship
                and scrawled its spirals
from Genoa Amsterdam
        Londonopolis each imperial canto
                unspooling a bit
broader than the last
        and each with its own forms
                and its own anxious fogs
from the Mediterranean
        nebbia to the sound
                swallowing mist squatting
on the Damrak Canal
        to the brume air of the nineteenth
                nervous century meeting
the yellow smoke of London
        like a little bookkeeper grown old
                and now the dead
white fog of Suisun Bay
        midmorning amid metaphors
                of the Pacifico
where a weary hegemon
        heaves up on Benicia's beaches
                ten thousand cars
paratactically abandoned
        ten thousand Sebring Sedans
                and Explorers

and Pontiac G8s and in oxide
                    orange a single Challenger
                                  that last hoplite
of American heavy metal
                  and they all hunch
                          in the weak sun too tired
to launch into the circuits
                  and some say this is a crisis
                              of overproduction
and some say
              this is a crisis of accumulation
                      and some say this is the most
beautiful sight the dark earth offers
                and some say
                      they should all be driven
into the Pacific
          like the end of *Jules and Jim*
                  ten thousand times over
in hopes we can start
            again in the factorial haze
                  of the Pearl River Delta
among the TVEs and the pop
           up cities or maybe
                we'll be rescued by
the new totalizers from the moon
           but as the formula
                    sinks downward to darkness
on extended credit
       discouraged and disemployed
                  I have heard late the chants
of the option-wallahs
       and the end of days
              traders and the armchair
Austrian fanboys singing
       marginal songs
              in the comment fields of the republic
where the endgame
       of the lyric turns to the language
              of value and who will take

the owners of debt

        and make them whole

                and who will take the shareholders

and make them whole

        and who will take

                the debauched and defaulted

and make them whole

        and who will take

                our brothers and sisters in the equity

and the mezzanine tranches

        and make them whole

                and when will this end and really

what will be money's Jena

        punctuated by crash

                and stink of counterparties unwinding

their positions in black bile

        and eurodollars

                in the unconfined unreckoned year

the cut throat of value speaks

        my name is Prince Valiant

                I have come from the capital

The Fire Sermon

1. RED EPIC

Mediators! matadors!
　　　　　　　how trivial and objective this world is!
　　　　　　　　　　　　　　　　　semiologists! stevedores!
how objective and trivial!
　　　　　　　equally fucked we are
　　　　　　　　　　　　　well not equally I have an MCM
aesthetic and a radio-controlled
　　　　　　　　　　death drive there are two parties
　　　　　　　　　　　　　　　　　　　to every romance
the waged and the wager
　　　　　　　　　and it has been getting harder
　　　　　　　　　　　　　　　　to decipher the difference
a throw of the dice will
　　　　　　　　　never reveal the real subject
　　　　　　　　　　　　　　　　oh mediators! stevedores! etc.

Madrid is sometimes in flames
　　　　　　　　　　though confusingly the Spanish
　　　　　　　　　　　　　　　　　　Stairs are in Rome
which is often in flames
　　　　　　　　　Oakland is sometimes pleasingly in flames
　　　　　　　　　　　　　　　　　　Athens is almost
always aflame also Thessaloniki
　　　　　　　　　　Big Data murmurs to me
　　　　　　　　　　　　　　　the likelihood that at a given

profit rate in a given sector
          a given household debt
                    a given wage deflation a given
neighborhood would be
          in flames given fire is the unfettered
                    substance of the situation

To begin again from the beginning
          to write only for one's friends
                    two lovers make a zero
two speculations make a hedge
          if *Tender Buttons* had been
                    written by capital instead of
OBJECTS FOOD ROOMS
          it would have a single section
                  called LABOR POWER
though technical language is not conducive
          to enlisting popular support
                    if *Lunch Poems*
were the poetry of the future
          it would be all like
                  I communize this I communize that

2. TRANSISTOR

There will be a revolution or there will not. If the latter these poems were nothing but entertainments. If the former it will succeed or fail. If the latter these poems were better than nothing. If the former it will feature riots fire and looting and these will spread or they will not. If the latter these poems were curiosities. If the former it will feature further riots manifestos barricades and slogans and these will leap into popular songs or they will not. If the latter that's that. If the former these popular songs will be overcome or they will not. If the latter these poems were no different than the songs. If the former the popular itself will be abolished via riots barricades manifestos occupations and fire or it will not. If the latter we will spend several more decades talking about culture. If the former the revolution will at this point be destroyed from within or without. If the latter these poems went down fighting. If the former it will feature awful confrontations with former friends and there will be further manifestoes new slogans ongoing occupations and communes and lovers will be enemies. We do not know what will happen after this point but surely this is enough to draw some preliminary conclusions. The poem must be on the side of riots looting barricades occupations manifestos communes slogans fire and enemies.

3. POEM ENDING WITH A LINE FROM NIEDECKER

I keep my mind under my arm
              where I hold my
                      head when I walk
down to market when I
            walk when I walk down
                  to the market
the actions are social
          but the mind is private
                when I walk down walk
down to the inferno
         the mind is private I had
               a vision the mind
is privately held
        under my arm when I
            walk I had a dream had a
Baudelaire had a
       Rimbaud the action is
           social but Apollinaire walks
down he promenades down
          to market promenades
             in the market
walks out walks home
        walks through streets named after
              market towns

the names are social
                        but the century is private
                                        the inferno is social
but the mind follows
                    the head thinks we can leave
                                        thinks we can go
down to the market
                    and leave just leave thinks we can
                                        be in it but not of it

You know all too well
                    that the best poetry is not
                                        the least revolution
you know also that poetry
                    is the best way available to you
                                        to affirm this truth
now we start to see how
                    the trap is sprung how it was
                                        sprung and all
before you were born
                    mind under your arm
                                        in the poetry market that exists
despite the spontaneous
                    wailings of the poets who believe
                                        there must be no
market because they
                    cannot afford that for which they
                                        should not have to pay
the action is social but the market
                    exists as the secret
                                        police exist alas the market
will never send you
                    to jail for your poems though
                                        we all believed in
private that we were
                    worth jailing for the terrible
                                        sedition of our dithyrambs
believed we deserved this honor
                    in a ¡NO PASARÁN!
                                        todos somos Pussy Riot

sort of way yet the good
          reader geared for riot zipties dangling
                    cometh not for us

The world of the poem is
          the world the world is abstract
                 and real the poem
fails just when it is victorious
           because one cannot live
                  the absolute of Victory
over the Sun until
         one can and we do and many
                will die when this happens
poetry will be renewed
          in the blood of the negative
                  "and dreadfully much else"

Tranche 1

I have lived through the end of syntax I have lived though the imperial grammars I have lived through the bursting of a bubble visible from space I have lived through the suicide of money to preserve the life of value I have lived through the fatal sacrifice of philosophy to avoid the jaws of the dialectic I have watched the spiral of Vico become the spiral of Sismondi and then watched that become le vrai viral livre I have stood atop a small hill with Mallarmé in one hand and in the other a cognitive balm and of what virtue were our pretty phrases against a thousand beautiful men standing in rank near the sunlit shore

Tranche 2

We have given our hearts away we have given away all our dollar-denominated assets including our hearts we like regular anarchy we like rational derangement we we we so excited we say contradiction is the fluid in which we are suspended we turn and return and turning is the form contradiction takes when we are drifting we turn round and round in the night we are citizens of the turn we are *tropolitan* and in the city of the turn in the moving contradiction we haven't really eaten or slept in a couple days and the men are beautiful and the women are beautiful and we remember that we meant to come here and never leave we meant this over and over but it meant something else

Haecceity

If what you want is calm
to be restored you are still the enemy
you have not thought thru clearly
what that means

if what you want is a national
moment of silence the indictment
of a single police officer
or two or three you are still
the enemy you have chosen the reverie
of law for you and your friends if you want

another review panel a Justice Dept
study a return to democracy rather than
for riot and looting to leap beyond
itself from county to county
rift to rift until it becomes general
you have not understood
what a revolution is it's just this

it's coming out again night after night more of us
than there are of them it's saying no
to every deal remember nothing
belongs to you because
nothing belongs to anyone

Spring Georgic

Listen I have something to tell you and it's too simple to tell it simply so

1872 Dostoyevsky publishes *Besy*
                           1913 Constance Garnett publishes first
English translation as *The Possessed*
                           so precisely within the brackets
of the Great War and the Commune
                           "human character changed"

A library is more like a palace than it is like a bookstore
                                       a bookstore is more
like a hotel
           a hotel is only something like a library
                                       but a great deal like a
department store
               while the department store and the high palace are one

Around that time we were leaving
                           behind realism and with it the struggle
over the working day
                   once that catastrophe was confirmed
                                       the fighting
shifted to the front of consciousness and
                                       then we were finally modern

In the main hall of the century the décor was a jumble of americanoiserie

I have read a lot of thick books
                        and become convinced of only three things

Do not send your army into Afghanistan
                        the Hindu Kush will swallow them

No matter the circumstance
                        do not grant emergency powers to anyone

I promise to finish but first an interlude on the romance of the lost manuscript

The *Passagen-werk* and *Theorie du speculation*
                        were both left to languish
in the National Library in France
                        while everybody was having modernism
and then recovered in the Fifties
                        and each book invented a new capital
one for the nineteenth century
                        one for the future of finance
                        oh those banky boys
swanning through the age of arbitrage
                        like hookers through the dizzy atrium
of the Hotel Future Foretold
                        and in São Paulo there is a department store
without any doors at all
                        what thoughts I have of you tonight Fred Jameson!

We make our plans among ruins
                        of the geopolitical baroque
                        at some point
we were all working downtown in bookstores
                        what a luxury!
                        like Coca-Cola
for breakfast
                        we took turns sitting on the floor
                        behind the back counter

reading new arrivals
        I remember *The Andy Warhol Diaries*
                      I remember
Lipstick Traces
        I remember all those black pocketbooks from Semiotext(e)

Now everyone is superflux
        but like credit we are
                getting ahead of ourselves

Later it would be translated as *The Devils* or *Demons*
                the Russian word *besy*
actually indicating spirits
        which may possess a body uninvited
                but are not
themselves possessed
        it seemed like a crude mistake had been rectified

To say it is a new era is to say
        it has discovered a new style of time
                we do
not do this in language
        first but in terrain we have not chosen and do not yet
understand
        language meets us there and must be cajoled
                into open air
by dangling the old forms
        in their wrack and wreckage
                this is the poetic thought

What true act would make every word in the dictionary political
                Nina says
book-burning and that seems right
        and it may be that a people can be judged
by how they answer this question
        and this too is the poetic thought

Lautreamont
        "mysterious and extreme Romantic"
                already in 1870 dead

in a hotel a few yards from where I stayed last week

                             Les Chants de Maldoror

largely unknown

               until it was discovered in a bookstore 1917

                                Hey Paris

you are beautiful but you are terrible at keeping track of books

                                  it had been

filed in the mathematics section

                  and finally this too is the poetic thought

Like credit the book is unable to be

                   in the same time with itself

                             its meanings

run ahead while it lingers on a shelf

               or its meanings come

                        racing to catch up

to the instant when the book is found

               in some poor agent's hand

                      and so

we are always naming

             the wayward motion of things

                     en route to realizing

themselves

        the fate   the itinerary   the defile   the fortune

But is there not a kernel of truth

               concealed within Garnett's error

                      if we speak

you and I of the dispossessed

            free and doubly free

                 to haul their flesh to market

why would we not call those others

             within whom moves the spirit of money

why would we not call these

          the possessed

              green and gold in the springtime

In March and in April and in May

             especially in late March

                 seize the fucking banks

The Transformation Problem

He died unable to lift himself above the shoals of everyday life.

This is the sin of despair.
>   I speak of course of Mayakovsky.

In the twentieth century the best you could say of a person was this.

The revolution betrayed him
>   before he betrayed the revolution.

Sappho the truth is the part.

You were the last love poet for a long time.

It was in this period that the idea of communism was born.

I like the Canto where Ezra tries to fuck a rock.

Pasolini loved the party from his youth.
                                    He preferred the boys with
smooth cheeks.
                    He had to leave Friulia
                                    to become the Friulian poet.
I think this is a tale of heresy.
                            In Rome they also had boys and the party
but with a difference—
                        no more unoccupied afternoons
                                            and many alleys.

Perverts and militants learn to keep other relations to windows.

Anyway they kicked him out and only then did he become a true communist.

You will see a theme developing.
                        We realize ourselves and die
                                            in exile.

The party got older and it began to take odd jobs and grow a beard.

This beard was Stalin.
                    In Rome boys with jaws cool and mean enough to survive
the years of lead to come.
                        Stalin's beard ruined it for everyone.

Ovid saw this simple fact early on.

                      We are subject to invisible and
impersonal forces.

           They go to work on us.

                          We flail in our chains.

The work of the world transforms the body over and over.

Things in nature seem more concrete

                      than humans with their airy discourse
but when spirits hum in every rock and river

                      the situation is reversed.

To undergo the metamorphosis

                into a tree among trees

                      is to become
more abstract and more free.

             This combination is lost to us now
thus the strange illumination

           of Ovid's words.

                 The transformations continue.

Little Object Andy

...playing a theremin
For the firemen

The cold of electricity caught
In the warmth of thought

The enigma of presence
The autonomy of absinthe

O to be haunted
To be Lautreamonted

Iambic tune that has no words it means
"This sad life all spectacle and no dream"

(Polis is metro polis is akros)

Polis is metro polis is akros
And the metro police have stenciled
Upon their shields ΑΣΤΥΝΟΜΙΑ

Polis is metro polis is akros
The acropolis has a balustrade
And here I sang city city city

Polis is metro polis is akros
We could no longer talk about talking
We wanted for another way forward

Polis is metro polis is akros
Here in the city-state of exception
Everything is at the mercy of

Everything else and all prices are found
In others in our sunwarped catextrophe

Gilded Age

Working from a text we can say that they are not allowed to travel
Working from a text we can say this poem may be a kind of betrayal
Working from a text we can say that they have had their tools taken away
Working from the text we must avoid any kind of poignancy
Working in a town where there are many car dealers and fewer charms
Or not working in a town because no tools and so just having a soda agrume
And reading from the Library of Riots and all of this seemed to some a special effect
And to the rest of us like life and like life part of it was made from texts

AGAINST THE DAY DEMON ONE WONDER FACTORY ORIGINAL GANGSTER STRAIGHT OUTTA
COMPTON ON A GENERATION THAT SQUANDERED ITS POETS SOUTH ASIA JE EST UN AUTRE
TRANCHE DE MEZZANINE NINA AND ALBERTO TOTAL SYNTAX SYNTAGMA SQUARE QUEER
SUBSTANCE STANCE OF CRITIQUE TIQQUN THE CALL CALL IT THOUGHT THOUGHT IS THE
BRIDE OF WHAT THINKING KING OF MAY MAYA ARULPRAGASAM GESAMTKUNSTWERK WORK-
DAY DAVID HARVEY VO OSEZ JOSEPHINE PHENOMENOLOGY OF SPIRIT WRITTEN EXAM MATISSE
BACKWARD IS SYSTEM TIM ON THE COVER OF THE CHRONICLE CALIFORNIA GURLS EARL'S
COURT 24 CITY EU EURODOLLAR LA ROUX RUE DES PYRAMIDES MIDDLESEX OCCUPATION ON
THE ROAD TO ROUEN ON CERTAINTY NTM M.PHIL FILM SOCIALISME METHOD THE DOLLAR
CRISIS ISIDORE DUCASSE CASSER DU SUCRE SUR LE DOS DE QUELQU'UN

A thing like a frag
A thing like a syn
A thing like a tag
a -ma   a -ment   a metatag and the fire in the bank

If an image disappeared its place was immediately filled with a kind of neutral plastic material we knew as the social stuff. And a new image would appear elsewhere with a gentle whoosh because the visible kept a careful equilibrium. Except it wanted to expand and sometimes when you woke in the morning there would also be an unfamiliar image where an old image had been and we didn't know if these were pasted one image on the other like an old billboard or if the new image covered over the social stuff or maybe it was what the stuff had become. The images were beautiful and often included clouds or words and word-clouds were themselves an allegory for the social stuff and like all allegories it went both ways. It was getting all over us.

Working from a text I felt guilty for working

You walk out the door and you're just like what's up global underclass?

We knew it was time
We knew it was time to leave
We knew it was time to leave our time
Love could not help with this

And all this talk of zones of ambience is possible because you live in a quarter that is the Jewish quarter in a neighborhood that is the queer neighborhood on a street that is mentioned by name in Zone just 98 years ago it is the street with the lesbian bars and this was the garment district at one point 95% of the nation's clothing made here and now it is fashionable as life is fashionable and at 9:30 AM the people who are almost beautiful enough to never work arrive for their jobs and it is the second day of spring measuring not by the calendar but the pleasure index of the air and you think this is close enough to be an image of your life as you are almost beautiful that is to say not beautiful and though you are professionally lazy you will never be free of the work and no one is transformed as the world is transformed and finally in the afternoon with pheromonal halos around their bodies the neighbors race out of their apartments to bang into each other on the corner and I want to be honest about how much I love this all of this and its pleasure is my pleasure and its wine is my wine when I can afford it and I am holding this in mind as truth and measure when I say it must be annihilated not as text but really now.

An age which no longer loves poetry has betrayed itself
There are not two kinds of poetry there is only one: Jacobin and unyielding
The first principles must be beyond dispute
The best poetry will have contempt for its era but so will the worst

It must be made from everything

including text—this is the minimum formula for realism—
but it does not align itself
with texts—it must align itself with work—meaning hatred
of work—it must desire
change so much it is accused of being in love
with annihilation—
must in fact love annihilation—the rest is sophism—

(It was raining in das Kapital)

It was raining in das Kapital
                    it was raining in the City
                                    population 111,000
in 1631 current population
                    eight thousand souls.
                                    It was raining in das Kapital
it was raining in the City
                    at the busy intersection
                                    of many great circles.
And maybe you are
                    a serotonin-slathered neuron
                                    crackling synapse to synapse
or a eurodollar riding the infosphere
                    toward the City
                                    or away which is also
toward the City.
          This is the majesty of a great circle.
                                    How every departure
also inaugurates a return
                    and whoosh you're back
                                    in das Kapital in the rain
in an abstract process and hot
                    money and music
                                    sounds better with you.

Come with me under the shadow
                    of this Northern Rock.
                                        There is a year exactly
between this poem and 1789
                    we thought it was 1900
                                        but it was MCM′ again.
O Latin alphabet O Roman
                    numerals O Greek tragedy
                                        you are with us now.
It was raining in the City
                    it was raining in das Kapital
                                        and we ran through
the landscape until
                    we bumped into a book
                                        within a book and whoops
there goes a Borsalino
                    whirling away comically
                                        down the rainrunnelled revenue.
It's a book of philosophy.
                    It is shy and carries
                                        a rag and a coke bottle
and with its free hand
                    gestures along one
                                        of the many great circles
that span outward
                    from this rainy spring corner
                                        and says what
every philosophy book
                    means to say come I am
                                        on my way to Syntagma.

(We lived in a cloud of recklessness)

We lived in a cloud of recklessness south of Market in a house with an accent when he said Taylorism it sounded like terrorism we lived in a cloud of restlessness and felt ourselves to be adrift east of China west of France south of Market north of Chance we lived in a fog of remorselessness in a long wave in a K-wave we sang I'm going back to Cali to Cali to Calligrammes we saw the world through world-colored glasses it was a situation known as snowglobalization down there south of the Market in a cloud of recklessness on a sea of credit and correlation in the winter of the long wave in the deep sea swell of the Market and the candidates threw roses and we ate the roses in the jaws of the present as we once ate Robespierre's raspberries

The Event

Talking to strangers about ZIDANE.

Talking to Michael and Geoffrey about ZIDANE.

Walking down the street but thinking about ZIDANE.

Sitting in a bar in a beur neighborhood discussing ZIDANE.

Listening to Adrienne Rich at the Village Voice July 18 but thinking about ZIDANE.

Listening to the new song about ZIDANE.

Imagining an entire book about ZIDANE.

Shopping for books but thinking about ZIDANE.

Sexual fantasies about ZIDANE.

People outside watching television through the window for news about ZIDANE.

Mentioning the Nitzschean Superman in re ZIDANE.

Appearance on the street of graffiti about ZIDANE.

And t-shirts and magazines about ZIDANE.

Drinking about ZIDANE.

Trip to the airport about ZIDANE.

Sleeping late about ZIDANE.

No summer and no ZIDANE only summer about ZIDANE.

Fab, Beta, Equity Vol

Option-ARMs and the man I sing who first
came from Detroit-Berlin into Black-Scholes

flight to liquidity flight to safety flight to quality

Real city derelict house derelict storefront
ostalgia for the productive forces
dude that's not emptiness it's abstraction
asserting itself on the home front now
who will love in your hollowed carapace

Dilution of violence and grief
spread over centuries to come
a lamentation congealed and spent
in the orgiastic present

credit is a form of fortune
telling that is always right
except in what kind of story

"The engine of history"
arose as a phrase
in a blue century long
afternoon before this
motordämmerung now
the velocity of risk
passing through us
and coming out as
filter disco ghettotech
panta rhei of finance being

The world which extruded six story apartment blocks
and warehouses of brick and filthy glass which made
making and finally faded when we used the word
real behind the back of consciousness we meant that
we meant industry and the industrial age you want
a total philosophy well there is my metaphysics

Galactic

And the neighbors are playing a recorded muezzin into the courtyard
And the people upstairs are having a party and laughing out the window
And the women are arriving in sparkly silver shoes
And the style I am told yesterday in London is called Galactic
And it was over last month says Bigna tan and beautiful with Romansch accent
And I am feeling very global about all of this we talk Borges translations
And catch up on the very latest fashions and is that not paradise?
And home again the next day I run into Damon and Naomi in the street
Stopping over en route to a wedding in Morocco it doesn't even feel coincidental
And we discuss Japanese noise bands and later I go to the leftist bar with wifi
Near the bookstore and the blue clouds and is that not paradise?
And thinking is a feeling too but one that cannot come to rest in another
And I am in love with everybody which is miserable and lasts
Five minutes amidst this great muchness of things I go down
To the noodle shop to act out scenes from a Wong Kar-Wai movie
In my head about which the sweet-faced counterman probably has no idea
Though he gives me some knowing looks and we are waiting together
In the noodle steam and in the tamarind and lemongrass steam
For an international letter with a key folded inside or for love to return
And in walks a sexy boy with scarred lip and WE ARE THE POWER t-shirt
And he is tremendously real just as abstract ideas are real and the absence
Of beloveds is real and the incomparable Faye Wong having of late
Moved to Beijing from the real world of the movies is still exactly as real

As the steam in the noodle shop is real and how is this not paradise?
If love is for the one if love is a redoubt against the many it is useless to me
It is some holiday and my friends are scattered like confetti on the earth.

(In the city it was warmer)

In the city it was warmer and things were starting to melt

We were feeling massively multiplayer but not the police

Everywhere the poetics of currency float even in the poetry

It was when I could no longer order my memories

That they became like memories rather than my life

Something was having trouble ending my country the century my headache

A friend is a fistful of funeralbarbitol and some others

Downtown uptick in romance languages as the dollar tanks

We left datatrails as we hurried through the diorama of the day

A twentyfour hour exposure from geosync orbit

Shows the objective form of consciousness it looks like shipping lanes

Facts modeled in three or four dimensions but not a story

We went to jail we were stupefied by what people did

Mostly to each other the minimum formula for materialism is

I didn't want to tell the story of the world but it kept making me

In the scattered forms of money we were feeling vernacular

End of empire waisted gowns and all this beauty listen hate

Grand narratives all you want but shopping is still a total system

Therefore total war or the adventure never begins

(*This town is going out of business*)

[This town is going out of business that I call my brain] [the public space of my head got suburbed] [the heaven-heaped core of capital-] [ized stars is empty now as sleep is full] [of new words for new feelings like infrastructure-] [nostalgia or love-outside-the-citadel] [the past tense is tragedy while the present tense is comedy] [as all the empires and epochs have ended] [but for this one and then only out here] [in the late districts of the imagination] [in the old light of our pretty periphery]

Apology

Oh capital let's kiss and make up
And I'll take back all those terrible things I said about you
To my friends and in poems. What do poets know
Of capital anyway? It's exhilarating the daily life of money
As it shifts and deliberates like Frank O'Hara buying gifts
In a haze of cosmopolite thirdworldism en route to a weekend
Out of town yet so affectless this becomes itself a signature
Affect. Via the artifice of the Dow Jones you often appear
To be in New York but I suspect that if consciousness is a story
You are in charge of narrative structure and so the Nasdaq
And the Footsie and Nikkei index cannot be said to *happen*
Any more than sentences happen. Like true feelings
You are everywhere at once. That's Neoplatonism
For you or simple immanence but either way the road leads
To St. Augustine and don't get me started. Nice city. Good job.
It must be hard to hold the things of the world in an order
While studiously skirting the question of whether you yourself
Are a thing and I can imagine the anxiety this causes but capital
Don't you ever lie on the couch near the coffee in the late morning
Flipping through a magazine you picked up in one of your
Supermarkets in California until you come to a photo
Of Britney Spears in flip-flops and drag—you know
Sort of like googling yourself? Just to verify your own
Existence in real life. What a relief. Could poets

Ever hate idealism as much as you do? No ideas but in
Money. Thus your sweetness: the portability and persistence
Of ideas that have given us so much pleasure and move
As pleasure must move through the gold integument
Of this life. Oh to be form's content. Capital on behalf
Of myself and all my friends I want to apologize
For you know 1917 and hope we can put that behind us
And do whatever it takes to feel joined to everyone else
In this town and distant cities and every person in the system
That is at this time and in this space of flows the world.

Omnibus Omnia

It's always a good day for Apollinaire and September too
And the public market's thatched awning barely remembers
It was once an arcade and I am in love with Green Gartside
Who is the most enigmatic pop star until the next one!
This is the replacement you get offered for your childhood.
Gone now those golden summers goofing off in Bretton Woods
But no time for melancholy when the California sun is emptying
Its bank account and the sidewalks are full of citizens bemusedly
Lining up to be alive and later there's a Zhang Ziyi movie
Playing down at the Panorama that wasn't there yesterday.
A small change but—could this be the crisis we hoped for?
Or just a cyclical correction like the rise and fall of hemlines?
"A new prince should make everything new" appeared
Within a Florentine discourse written the same decade
As *Utopia* before returning as three small words MAKE IT NEW
Now spread like a stain across the long twentieth century
But that can be our little secret and a lesson in humility for the new
Confucians—culture happens everywhere at once or not at all
And *we* belong to *it*. In France the France you see on television
The latest styles are on the march down the Faubourg St. Honoré
Around the corner from the sunny plaza where they once cranked
The guillotine. Twice a year fashion kills itself and walks again
Though no one's saying that's a theory of history or anything but
Where are the skinny black suits of yesteryear? Oh they're back

For a few minutes in the fall and this cycle of revolution and return
Calls everything to the instant and Apollinaire is walking around again
And Villon is riding around like Carina Lau who is riding around again
In the punctual train from the future that still hasn't arrived
And the sans-culottes and Scritti Politti are walking around again
But we are walking around for the first time! Me and you
Before these wonders for the first time and Stephanie
And Mei-mei saying hello inside the system of objects
Also for the first time! Having been born and still Utopian
We race off to the revolutions of the Marc Jacobins!

The Red Posters

We had been in the world for a while and two men stood on opposite platforms conversing loudly in a language while they waited for their trains, and these were our trains too, we shared the trains as we shared the news, we followed the image-trails down to our image-defeats and we shared these too, there was always some defeat or the occasional image-victory on television or the covers of the dailies, *a Lib and a Trib*, this was our daily regime, and trains and language and money were the main ways of moving things into distance and time, O our century that we lived in like a city.

We had been in the world for a while, image-wounded, image-lit, we talked across the tracks, we had reasons for staying, we were hunched in the metro within the great circulation, red posters hung on the walls, they seemed to announce further defeats in cryptic terms, the main feeling on the platform was hardly a feeling at all, the sensation of the circuits routing through us, it was the way of being in the world we had been offered, and not being able to name it was part of this, when we hung posters they were world posters, the images hurt or betrayed us and we did the same to them, finally we lived together in the image-world.

A train came, the conductor leapt off the front car as another leapt on to replace her, and the first conductor swung her bag of street clothes as she climbed the stairs out of the station, the beauty of this was our beauty too, it was world beauty, the men stood on platforms that were world platforms and though they appeared poor they lived here with us, in a world city, we were world men and world women, the trains were world trains, when we spent money it leapt right into the circuits, whoosh, we saw right away that it had been in our care but it didn't belong to us, it was world money.

Memories of Bergen op Zoom

What if there wasn't another way
                  but this one
                            turned out to be different
enough? The film
              ran at different speeds
                         in different places in the world
system
        and here they wore Margiela and here
                          they invented baile funk.
The grinding of zones against zones
                    gave forth a gout of sparks
                           we called
spirit and sometimes
             it appeared to come to rest
                      inside mute things
like poems
      but this was a famous illusion.
                    Swallowed by the dream
of factories we vomited forth
           the factory of dreams.
                    Leaving the twentieth
sentence
     was taking longer than expected
               with our train clacking along

in its sprockets and though
                    we had been traveling a while
                                        in the distance
you could still see the departure station
                              waving in evening—
                                        another night
spent on the Brecht-Bardot Line
                      waiting for the reversal
                                        that would set it all
on its feet again.
                Not the history of violence
                              but the violence of history.
The poets are reading
                  Machiavelli when they should be
                                        reading Clausewitz.

(Stop it with your strategies)

Stop it with your strategies. The longest social experiment in history
Has been abandoned, nobody liked it anyway, the cigarettes were awful.
Now we live in cities where daily life is so sensual one retreats
Into abstraction. Dirty canals, cars on fire, autumn. Under the glass and iron
Of the train station bar the train station pigeons fly into your hair.
You listen to a song no one will remember in 30 months, no one
But this poem, this decay of the little event that happens at the point
Of purchase. People are departing or arriving, it's impossible to tell
By looking, like the duckrabbit that so amused the twentieth century
Philosophers. The mind as we know it was developed in winter gardens,
Panoramas, factories, wax museums, casinos, train stations—O architecture
You are the greatest art, your content is modernity! I am an incarnation of time,
I do not own my own weapons, when I go to the movies to cure my boredom
I do not wish to see boredom represented, take that French film-makers,
You've taken everything else, the Pop Years is over, here comes China.

Le Mépris

"Basically it's a movie about Bardot's ass and the rest is chit-chat," in three colors, at Cinecittà, at Casa Malaparte, in the middle with the togas and wigs in the apartment the couple can neither afford nor leave, in the housing bubble that holds them so tenderly, the long boom, the apartment in the city tossed like a pebble into world, the Sunday of the world, where everything can be summed up in aesthetics and political economy, and the movies are everything, and poetry is everything, and the call of the Siren has become merely the wistful longing of the passer-by, this has happened in history, but history isn't something.

Contempt

This illuminated surface of events, this present tense, this staring at screens we have been doing to escape the flatness of these deadpan days. This calling movie dreams, this calling memories Rome. The colors in *Contempt* come from a world with more minutes in each hour, but a real world, a world almost remembered in this long celebration of a cult without dreams and without mercy. O record stores and union halls, O leaded-glass nostalgia for an artisanal form of this catastrophe. O recollected thickness of that one newspaper Franco calls "the daily of my life," O le cleft chin de Jack Palance, O world where Coca-Cola has not lost its true flavor.

LTCM

1. CENTURY

O local details so favored by poets chronicling the foot traffic of reality and all these toy sums changing hands.

O arc'd abstractions that glow along the curve of the globe also revered by poets.

O the itch to make an account of it all.

To tell the story of my century and how it ended.

Of my friends and brawls and the Asian Flu and Long-Term Capital Management.

Of books and books and you know who's beautiful language.

Of my century from dada to Prada.

Of my century that began in the end you are tired of this modern world.

Of the century that ended when I wrote this poem on the day Jean Baudrillard died with opulent spring just a week away.

O opulent spring o century o bituaries.

I loved noodle stands home-made poetry books songs no one would admit to liking the reverie of the negative decrepit movie houses Vicodin stock market crashes and the streetsigns in fifteen cities.

What were once facts are now feelings.

Horace mentions the tears of things and we would like to set out a bowl of milk and coax this idea into the theater of the present.

Meaning flows backward from the period so the century ends before it begins.

What were once facts are now feelings and so we bid farewell to the swans and manifestoes and the swans in manifestoes.

I loved the palindrome and the ourobouros and the subway system turning back on itself.

Century where I salted my heart with the money of the absolute!

2. ENVOI TO CENTURY

Century without Rimbaud that cherubic jerkoff at the corner of the table.

Century did you have to return Rimbaud as Howard Hughes?

Century of the new tears of things.

Dream of the subject and object aligning.

Century can't we get it over with and just start calling this *the sobject?*

3. CITY

O opulent spring just a week away!

Spring where we go out into the system of systems.

Go out into the nodes and the pathways and the sun-green sun.

Out into our city where we came to live in close contagion with beloveds and strangers and neighbors-who-art-a-drag and so finally became organic.

Into our downtown which at evening empties of people and becomes form without content.

We meditate on pure form it arouses the most poetic emotions which turn at once to become dry motes of content.

But in the day in the sun-green sun we encounter the latest contagions the nerve transmissions that hold us we speak of Lil Wayne we speak of M.I.A. and the new songs of cities.

They are about us as buildings are about us in the downtown in the opulent spring.

O cities and the architects who invent new names for the situations like Bubble Cities and New Towns and Zoomburbs.

There is no shortage of names.

There is no shortage of names but basically there have been three kinds of cities Labyrinth Grid Sprawl four if you count the Network.

The Network for which Los Angeles was the rough draft and people lived there as they lived in the other orders no more nor less angelic.

They are all ways of knowing and each has its own metro system and preferred kinds of terrorism.

All of these can be found in history which keeps ending despite annual July Fourth backyard party ongoing Chez Juliana where the anarchists huddled near the back fence in memory of public space.

There I drank a drug in memory of my content.

In memory of you who might in another cycle in a later city feel the contagion of this poem as alone at dusk in the downtown's inky archive I felt the kind contagion of you.

O cities there is no city.

4. CINEMA

The world for a nickel, a knickknack for Makhno, a Malevich movie, a show of money, the money of the world, the rule of reverie, a breakaway republic of dreams, cinema is nothing, a flimsy excuse, sand castles and player pianos, a dime for your reverie, a nickel for your negation, cinema wants everything, the black army, the blank screen, the museum of the present, the abyss of apparatus, it was ending and it was going to end, 24 black squares a second...

5. SYSTEM

System climbs up on the *oikos* and starts to sing and this song is the epic and economy.

They don't write'em like that anymore.

What were once facts are now feelings.

What was once a vague sense of unease is now China.

Within *being* we are now inside *Beijing*

We make our way through a thicket of signs.

We make our way through buildings and stanzas and eras inside of which it feels a certain way.

What is that feeling and can we name the metro system after it.

Smeared with grime and system maps and advertisements for department stores and we make our way through a thicket of time.

Time which is form before form which we fill with linen and glass and manifestos and hot money and these are the new ages.

I love you as I love time itself because we share the same apples and amours and alephs the same bricks and bad faith and Beckett translations the same contagion and the charisma of the negative.

Though this has moved on to other stations.

Has moved on to HK cinema and Tamil disco and the universal newspaper of dreams where it is writ that economy is an epic without heroes.

And music is philosophy without proper names.

Still we are the words of others.

We are the words of others still unaligned still stumbling and uncertain having seen only the billboard for Utopia.

In the opulent spring unbuttoning its shirt and still no sign of the sobject.

In hypnotic sex and in liquidity flows and in the sun-green sun.

In the lonely hour of the last instance.

One must be indifferently modern.

6. LONG-TERM CAPITAL MANAGEMENT

The Thai baht glows briefly.

Even the old 50 baht with the Chapel of Wat Benchamabopit long-since bumped but still legal glows briefly.

The rupiah glows in Indonesia and we are skipping over the Malaysian ringgit the Philippine peso and the Singapore dollar's Orchid series its Bird and its Ship series.

The stations and the circuits between stations lighting up in a sequence so complex it's mystical or maybe it's like following a branching thought through the brain of it all—the System Entire which has no real name.

In the most tangled complexity one finds moments of great intimacy where the sun shines on a friendly picture of Soeharto with open collar and a jet rising reverse over Soekarno-Hatta Airport and so glows the Indonesian rupiah.

And the South Korean won 10,000 glows through the now-destroyed Water Clock of Borugak Pavilion with moiré on watermark and intaglio latent image.

And then the ruble which has been everywhere and once rubbed shoulders with Mayakovsky.

The ruble glows and starts to fade at the frontiers of Asia and now a pause in the series but comes a moment in which the effigy of the Republic and the green-winged

Macaw on their dusty rose perches inside the Brazilian 5 real note both glow briefly ever so briefly.

And the peso convertible the pride of Argentina on which appears in gentle blue the disgraced historian who first translated Dante into Spanish this too finally glows and that is said to be the end of beauty.

But I say there is nothing as beautiful as the yuan and among all the various bills with their lotuses and their Halls of the People none compares to the humble kuai note with its orchid watermark and Three Pools Mirroring the Moon at West Lake.

Metalipsis for Uyen Hua

As I have argued elsewhere most people are Rihanna
And the rest are Donald Sutherland or maybe
Michael Caine—whichever one was in *Alfie*.

I don't mean this typologically like there are
Two kinds of people. There are two people
In the world and they share certain things but

Have never met and we are them—all of us are
Them and this is okay. In fact I would give
My left eye to be the beautiful boy who was in *Alfie*

but I'm not I'm Rihanna. This is my flag
Of convenience when I am walking
With headphones on through the theory district.

Questions of the Contemporary

Immaterial labor. What is it
     really and the periphery. A system
         is not a solution.
Also does transport create
     value where there was none
         or is that just buying cheap
and selling dear. The next M.I.A.
     will it be terrible again.
         The next Robyn will it be
great again. Fall 2007 spring
     2005 we shall not look
         upon their like again. I'll show you
a god damned panegyric.
     Why do things end
         because teleology. The land will become
sea and so will be free
     sang the Dutch villeins. De Witte's picture
         of the world's
oldest bourse 1602 Amsterdam
     is in Rotterdam do you not
         see how this is a fucking
problem. Hi-Cube intermodal
     shipping containers used
         for shops Shoreditch also

homeless holding cells Elephant
                    and Castle. Surplus population
                                        and the arbitrage
of minor emotions. Hip-hop riots
                    and the space of flows is one
                                        talk I will never give
again. Straight hoodie and luxury
                    goods chorus Gucci Gucci Louis
                                        Louis Fendi Fendi
Nada. Some of our friends
                    were dating Leninists and
                                        that was weird. We should read
Vol. 2 again together srsly
                    so boring but babies are
                                        definitely Department III. Oh
And also? Reproductive labor. What is it
                    really and wages for house
                                        parties Oakland
I need an emoticon for lol
                    and flinching with dread
                                        simultaneously. Why do things
seem to shudder
                    because volatility. What if they figure out
                                        how to hedge against
like everything. COINTELPRO
                    tip: permanent counterrevolution
                                        needs quants!
A possibility is not a program.
                    Summary as of fiscal
                                        fourth quarter 2013 Kreayshawn
is not coming back. Production
                    is not coming back.
                                        Alan Sekula is not coming back.
Some big container ships are
                    coming back some are
                                        underwater. One standard
forty ft container equals two
                    twenty ft equivalent units
                                        or TEUs but so does one

Hi-Cube despite eight additional m³
                              it's not an exact science like
                                        Max Martin. Just a slab
of unfigured air a kind of
                    room to move. The desire
                                    of a planetary civilization three pct
maybe three five and enough
                    left over for the aesthetic.
                                        Annualize that shit. What if
it's just cruel mercantile
                    plus dubstep from here on out.
                                    What if it's just IF THE RICH
WIN THE LIVING WILL ENVY
              THE DEAD. Why do things keep on
                              because *reasons*.

ACKNOWLEDGMENTS

"Years of Analysis for a Day of Synthesis" is dedicated to the memory of Giovanni Arrighi (1937-2009), this book's Virgil. "Transistor" is for Ruth Jennison. "Little Object Andy" is for Andrew Joron. "Contempt" is for Franco Moretti. "Metalipsis for Uyen Hua" is for Uyen Hua. "Questions of the Contemporary" is for Sianne Ngai, time-comrade. "Haecceity" is a version of Diane Di Prima's "Revolutionary Letter No. 19"; that poem provides as well this book's epigraph.

Gracious thanks to the editors of the journals in which some of these poems first appeared, occasionally in different form: *The Baffler, The Believer, Columbia Poetry Review, Counterpath Online, Critical Quarterly, Denver Quarterly, Electronic Poetry Review, Jubilat, The Nation, Scythe, With + Stand*. Cal Bedient and David Lau at *Lana Turner: A Journal of Poetry and Opinion* have been unremittingly generous in publishing the first and last poems here, and several in between. Versions of some poems appear as well in *nY, Vacarme*, and *Grumeaux*. I am grateful to the translators, Els Moore and Piet Joostens in the former case, Abigail Lang in the two latter; Abigail in particular has provided parallax, company, and kindness. I am grateful to the Cornell Society for the Humanities, and while there, for the hospitality of Bruno, Simone, Lucas, and Manu. Special thanks to Tim Simons for his design work and advice. This book would not have been possible without Seeta Chaganti.

This writing came out of events and conversations shared with friends, especially those who passed through the oscillation that began c. 2007: ERA OF READING GROUPS, ERA OF HELICOPTERS, MORE READING GROUPS, MORE HELICOPTERS. All of these friends appear here in various ways, as do others who were always there in spirit. This is their book.